IMAGES OF ENGLAND

EASTBOURNE

IMAGES OF ENGLAND

EASTBOURNE

JOHN SURTEES AND NICHOLAS R. TAYLOR

TEMPUS

Frontispiece: Aerial view of Eastbourne *c.*1935, from the Crumbles shingle (bottom) to Beachy Head Downland (top).

First published 2005

Tempus Publishing Limited
The Mill, Brimscombe Port,
Stroud, Gloucestershire, GL5 2QG
www.tempus-publishing.com

British Library Cataloguing in Publication Data.
A catalogue record for this book is available from the British Library.

ISBN 0 7524 3682 1

Typesetting and origination by Tempus Publishing Limited.
Printed in Great Britain.

Contents

Acknowledgements

Our special thanks to our wives, Sheila and Siobhan, for their constant help and encouragement. Acknowledgements also to Brian Allchorn, Stanley Apps, Steve Benz, Wilf Bignell, Judith Brent, Stephen Brewer, Ann and Alan Caffyn, John Cant, Muriel Childs, Mavis Clack, John V. Claremont, Gordon Clark, Michael Clark, Betty and Arthur Cobb, Terry Connolly, J. and L. Davies-Gilbert, Peter L. Drewett, Dorothy Ecroyd, Bob Elliston, John Farrant, Ian H. Ford, Lawrence Ford, Paul E. Fulford, Roger and Jean Gordon, John Gowland, Alastair Graham, Clive Griggs, Stella Hardwick, Paul Harris, Ken Harrison, Ted Hide, Vera Hodsoll, Graham Household, Chris Howden, Frances Jardine, Lionel Jones, Chris Jordan, Derek Keay, W.H. Kefford, Harold and Sylvia Kennedy, Lorna Kenward, Norman Kinnish, Margaret T. Knight, Percy G. Langdon, Marie Lewis, Peter Longstaff-Tyrrell, Lou McMahon, Pauline Markquick, Robert J. Marrion, Rosemary and John Milton, Frances Muncey, Michael Ockenden, S.C. Nash, Miriam C. Nixey, Betty and Peter Palmer, Michael and Tim Partridge, Jack Putland, Nigel Quiney, John Redfern, Matthew Rowe, Brian Robinson, Harold D. Spears, John and Irene Stevens, Pat and Lawrence Stevens, Fran Stovold, D. Swift, Gillian Tarrant, Joan and Ken Thurman, Doreen Toghill, Betty Turner, Ronald Turner, Dr Kenneth Vickery, W.J. Vine, Jack Warne, Edgar Williams, Esther Worsfold.

Also to Beckett Publications; *Brighton Argus*; British Library; British Museum; Caffyn's Plc Publicity Department; University Library, Cambridge; Channel Photography; Eastbourne Local History Society; Eastbourne Town Council Minutes; Eastbourne Central Library; Eastbourne Natural History and Archaeological Society; East Sussex Public Record Office; Hastings Museum and Art Gallery; Imperial War Museum; Walter Llewellyn & Sons Ltd ROK; Museum of History of Science, Oxford University; National Portrait Gallery; Science & Society Picture Library; Royal Mail Stamps Marketing; Towner Art Gallery and History Museum; National Archive, Kew.

Any relevant individual or organisation which inadvertently has not been acknowledged is asked to accept the authors' apologies.

Introduction

No watering place on the southern coast is fairer than Eastbourne; none is so elegant in the disposition of its attractions.

Daily Telegraph, 14 December 1893

The seafront is the heart and lungs of any seaside resort and Eastbourne is blessed with exceptionally enhancing features, partly provided by mankind, such as a picturesque pier, a lack of Kiss-Me-Quick emporia thanks to the Duke of Devonshire's restrictive covenants, and the tiered Western Parades also commissioned by the Duke, a great attraction today and a miraculous achievement in the days of spades and wheelbarrows. Nature's contribution was merely to provide the ideal site for a thriving marina, safe bathing along the front, the protective, romantic majesty of glorious Beachy Head – the highest chalk headland on the South Coast – and the highest mainland hours of sunshine figures; well, usually.

The area has evidence of human activity from the Stone Age, and the Romans had a sumptuous villa just by the pier. The town did get a write-up in the Domesday Book but otherwise not much happened while the economy depended on agriculture, mainly sheep-grazing on the Downs, and a little fishing. Until, that is, the aristocracy tired of spas and gambling and decided that drinking sea water cleared you out more effectively. Bathing from Eastbourne beach is recorded in 1754 but the real impetus for the switch from farming to tourism was the royal visit of Prince Edward in 1780. He has been followed by almost everybody who was anybody, from Charles Dickens, Jenny Lind and Karl Marx to Lewis Carroll, Edward Lear, Claude Debussy, Rupert Brooke, Mabel Lucy Attwell and most of the royal family, intelligentsia and captains of commerce.

The town was also lucky in that the land was owned by just two rich families, the Cavendishes (Dukes of Devonshire) and the Davies-Gilberts. They were always ready to donate a site for a good cause, such as a church, and thanks to their sage approach the development of the town took place in an organised manner with an eye for changes which would meet with approval from discerning contemporaries and potential residents, to produce 'A town built by gentlemen for gentlemen'.

With the tourist in mind, the local council strove to keep out heavy industry and even when encouragement was given to factories, in order to reduce seasonal unemployment, it was a case of only clean businesses need apply.

The most important business in the town after tourism was the acceptable one of private education, and with alumni such as George Orwell, Alec Guinness, Cyril Connolly, E.M. Forster, Eddie Izzard, Prunella Scales, John Wells, and with two Nobel Laureates, it no doubt contributed the brains of the town – although we don't mention super-spy Kim Philby, head boy at the Aldro School in 1924. It is likely that in late Victorian times some 82 schools thrived in a town of 35,000 people. Many catered for the children of colonial administrators, although families moved to Eastbourne simply because of the choice of schools on offer. Most of the town's children, however, did not have such options and until 1902 had to rely on overcrowded church schools. Nowadays, only four private schools survive.

So not all of Eastbourne was 'select' and it has also had its share of murders and scandals which demand a reference.

Sport and other entertainments are essential components of a holiday and Eastbourne has its fill of theatres and restaurants. As for sport, we all know of the pre-Wimbledon women's tennis tournament at Devonshire Park and there is a quiverful of sports facilities, from famous golf clubs to a David Lloyd leisure centre. The oldest football team in the county, Eastbourne Town, play at the Saffrons, a famous ground for all sports which had a county cricket week for many years, and another soccer team, Eastbourne Borough, even made it to the play-offs for the Conference League in 2005.

As health-bestowing properties for the young, invalids and convalescents were a crucial element of any self-respecting resort, the medical scene merits a mention.

While the Carpet Gardens are famous around the world, the town as a whole continues to win accolades as Eastbourne in Bloom, with a mulitiplicity of colourful, enchanting spots and peaceful parks not to be missed.

Years of slumber hidden away from the world have been cast aside over the last two centuries; the town even had its first public electric light five hours before New York, and by the early 1900s it was the second largest town in East Sussex and a leading centre of aviation. In the Second World War it was the most bombed town on the South Coast and, although grievously mauled, it has regained its cachet as the Empress of Watering Places.

Despite many changes in the holiday scene, leading to the short break and a much greater reliance on the conference trade and product launches, Eastbourne's natural blessings (it had more sunshine hours then ever in 2003) combined with a happy mix of adapting to the new ways by means of events such as the annual *Airbourne* air show, without losing the ambience which makes it different, mean that it enters the twenty-first century with sure confidence.

There's a lot to see and discover in Eastbourne.

John Surtees and Nick Taylor
May 2005

one

The Seafront

Sovereign Harbour is a new and exciting part of Eastbourne. Covering 125 hectares (350 acres) with 65 acres of water and spaces for thousands of boats, it stretches from Langney to Pevensey Bay. If it isn't spoilt by overdevelopment, it should be much superior to other marinas further west along the coast. With a variety of shopping and dining experiences, it is popular with locals and sailors from Britain and Europe.

The swans have found a quiet corner of Sovereign Harbour but there is plenty to do here: trips around the bays, radio-controlled model boating and always the working of the locks, the fishermen with their catches, the remains of a Martello tower built to combat Napoleon's tricks, and many other activities.

A tiny part of the Sovereign Harbour marina. First mooted in 1962, Parliamentary approval was not received until 1980, when Tarmac and Asda bought the land from the Chatsworth Trustees. Work commenced in 1991 and on 19 February 1993 the barrier between the sea and the outer harbour was breached, allowing the tides to flood in and out. May 1993 saw the first boat sail through the lockgates to enter the inner marina.

Aerial view of Sovereign Harbour, 2002. The outer tidal harbour is protected by harbour arms of granite, brought by barge from Norway. An inner marina has residential and business developments. Eastbourne with its pier is in the middle distance and in the far west is the start of the Beachy Head cliffs.

Next along the front is the Sovereign Centre in Royal Parade, opened by Diana, Princess of Wales in June 1989. The east of the town was being developed on the Crumbles shingle; a swimming pool to replace the Devonshire Baths opened in 1977. For the official opening, the Sovereign Centre had a makeover with a training pool and a fun pool – slides and waves, loungers and floats thrown in – and in 2000 had another revamp. It now offers saunas, a gym, sunshowers and badminton.

Go past Fort Fun, Spray Water Sports, the Fishermen's Club and Treasure Island and you come to the grounds of the Redoubt, given by the eighth Duke of Devonshire in 1905. Between the wars, the Redoubt had a bandstand, bowling and putting greens and tennis courts. In 1968 the bandstand was replaced by a sun lounge, known since 1994 as the Pavilion Tea Rooms.

Grenadier and Scots Fusilier Guards camping at the Redoubt Fortress, 1865. The fortress was built from 1806 to act as a supply depot for the Martello towers as part of the defences against Napoleon; later it was used by many sections of the armed forces and coastguard. The casemates surround the central area, with gun positions on top. In 1924 the fortress was bought by the borough for £150 and opened to the public.

In 1940 the Redoubt was considered for an air-raid shelter but evacuation of most of the town's residents was adopted instead. From 1957 the Redoubt housed the model village (above with the casemates at the back) and later the Blue Grotto Aquarium. Now it is home for the museums of the Royal Sussex Regiment, Combined Services and, from 1988, the Queen's Own Irish Hussars.

Above left: In 1925 the council in a fit of madness deemed that telephone kiosks on the front should have thatched roofs to match the rustic public shelters. This kiosk was near the Redoubt. After 1936 the injunction was relaxed and the kiosks returned to their bald state.

Above right: Could this be a bizarre place to pile up a load of throw-away flotsam or is it a delightful artistic caprice using environmentally replaceable gems.

A floral tribute to a century of dedicated service by the St John Ambulance in one of the many small gardens along Marine Parade. Eastbourne has won many 'Britain in Bloom' awards.

The Redoubt surrounds have been livened up over the last decade. Above left: one of the early pier kiosks, which was found rotting in Manor Gardens/Gildredge Park and renovated, is installed in Pavilion Gardens. Above right: this ornamental seat adds a light attractiveness to the scene, and you can see the ex-kiosk in the background.

An early 1900s view of the pier showing the kiosk (on the left) now in the Redoubt Pavilion Gardens. Notice the sign advertising 'Animated Pictures Daily'; the first public films in Eastbourne were shown on the pier in 1903 but not as a regular feature.

Above: Grace, wife of Carew Davies-Gilbert (1852-1913). He played a substantial role in donating land and selectively developing his part of Eastbourne, which included much of the Crumbles and the east end of the town.

Top right: Frederick Gowland Hopkins (1861-1947). Born in Marine Parade, he watched the pier being built and cherished the hope that he could be involved in a great enterprise. He became Professor of Biochemistry at Cambridge, was knighted, elected president of the Royal Society 1930-35, and became a Nobel Laureate for his work on vitamins.

Centre right: December 2000 saw a ceremony for the re-siting of the 1865 drinking fountain from the corner of Seaside and Langney Roads to the new Seahouses Square.

Below right: Thomas Henry Huxley FRS (1825-95) expounded Darwin's theory of evolution and coined the word 'agnostic'. He resided in Staveley Road 1890-95.

Marine Parade, 1860. Although records of fishing families date back to 1296 and the Hide family have been traced back to the 1500s, Eastbourne, with its open beach, never had a substantial fishing fleet. Boats were launched at near high tide and run up the beach at high water and left beached. In 1594 John Norden noted that 'the fishermen spend what they get ... which decayeth the Towne'. Parish records name three fishermen drowned in 1605.

Most of the sailors who in summer plied 'Skylarks around the Bay' worked as fishermen – and lifeboatmen – in the winter. Here is a group spratting in the 1930s.

Edward Oliver painted this view of Marine Parade in the 1880s. Charles Darwin wrote part of his *Origin of Species* in the early 1850s while staying in Marine Parade.

Another stretch of Eastbourne's old seafront around 1885, including the Anchor inn (dating from the early 1800s at No. 20 Marine Parade), later named the Albermarle Hotel.

Opposite below: Splash Point. Even after the construction of a sea wall to the east of the pier, the waves would break over the wall in a south-west gale. Behind is the Queen's Hotel, opened in 1880 with Henry Currey as architect. The hotel was also a bulwark to divide off the eastern, working-class part of the town. Before 1939 no lady would be seen with a shopping basket on her arm, nor would she walk east of the Queen's Hotel. In the 1990s the hotel management removed the chimney pots, a measure greeted with such an outburst that they were hurriedly replaced.

Marine Parade in the early 1900s. The seaplane in the foreground looks about to take off on one of Major Fowler's joyrides along the front.

The seafront just by the pier, 1780. In the centre is the Round House where Prince Edward stayed that year for his successful holiday – like all Eastbourne vacations – and which set Eastbourne on course to become the Empress of Watering Places. He became the Duke of Kent, father of Queen Victoria, and Prince Edward Island in Canada is named after him. The Round House fell into the sea in 1841.

A memorial, seen here around 1906, to those of the 2nd Battalion Royal Sussex Regiment killed between 1882 and 1902. The statue, designed by Sir William Goscombe John, was unveiled by the Duke of Norfolk in 1906. Behind is Cavendish Place, where Friedrich Engels (1820–95) used to stay on his visits. At the time, all the Regency-style terrace balconies had decorative hoods.

View from the pier, 1950s. Holidaymakers are enjoying themselves all the way along Marine Parade. The tourist trade was good, the rush to the Costa Brava had not started and folk wanted to forget the war.

A view of Eastbourne from the pier head, *c.* 1900. The pier is 300m (1,000ft) long and mostly around 20m wide. The Queen's Hotel is on the right and the Grand Parade of 1851 to the left.

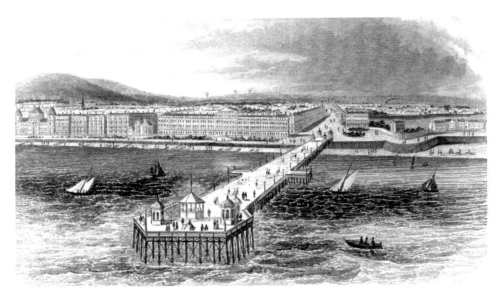

The Eastbourne Pier Co. was registered in 1865 with £15,000 capital. Built by Eugenius Birch, of Blackpool Pier and Brighton West Pier fame, for £13,500, the pier opened in 1870 and was completed in 1872, around the time of this engraving. It was intended to be a landing stage for coastal steamers, so there were no theatres or amusement arcades. A walk along the pier was considered rather daring and quite enough to make some Victorians distinctly queasy.

On New Year's Day 1877 a storm washed away the landward half of the pier. When it was repaired, the landward half was at a higher level and you can see the join to this day. The Carpet Gardens were just lawns and a hedge until acquired by the borough, when floral designs based on carpet patterns were introduced.

The pier, *c.* 1902. The pier head theatre was erected in 1901. The photograph also clearly shows the games saloons halfway along the pier, which were built around the same time.

Eastbourne Pier, *c.* 1912, with its sparkling new kiosks that lasted until 1951. Until 1926 no kiosk opened on a Sunday. Near the pier head is a passenger steamer plying the South Coast or over to France. 'For half-a-guinea we went to Boulogne on the *Devonia*, one of Campbell's paddle boats. There was a band playing and an observation platform to view the paddle-wheel pistons.'

The Music Pavilion (centre) was added in 1925-26 after the near part of the pier had been widened. It was converted into a dance hall when ballroom dancing was popular in the 1950s and is now an amusement arcade, with Funtasia and Waterfront. The end-of-the-pier theatre suffered an arson attack in 1970 but was soon back in business, and recently the camera obscura has been restored.

The pier in 2003, seen from the east and bathed in early morning light. It looks just as magical when outlined by fairy lights in the evening all through the year. The change of levels halfway along dates from when the near half was washed away in 1877.

Grand Parade, built in 1851, was the original project of the second Earl of Burlington (later the seventh Duke of Devonshire), as envisaged by his first architect James Berry, with gardens included. It was a financial flop: not only did all the builders go broke but the Duke couldn't sell any of the lots at auction. The Burlington Hotel occupied the main part by 1938 and the Claremont Hotel had the eastern end by 1951. Now the Burlington is owned by Wallace Arnold.

All through the year the Carpet Gardens are a riot of colour, enhanced by fountains and floral tableaux. The Carpet Gardens are only one part of Eastbourne in Bloom with its many parks and quiet spots. The gabled house in the centre was the Sussex Club (now Clive Court) where the Central Library was housed from 1946-64 after the bombing in 1943.

Looking west across the pier towards the distant Wish Tower in the early 1900s. At that time, the sailing or rowing boats were popular and three or four firms provided trips round the bay, but Allchorn's, founded in 1861, is the only one in business now, although the family retired in 1995.

This is the *Golden City*, one of the Allchorn boats, in the 1930s. She was the local lifeboat *James Stevens No. 6* before she was purchased by Allchorn's 'at enormous expense' and converted to carry passengers. She was billed as unsinkable and self-righting.

Above left: Each year in the summer the Langham Hotel exhibits this old bathing machine, striking in its bright yellow and ochre strips of colour.

Above right: A family group pose outside their bathing machine. The days when whole families came down to Eastbourne for the season, bringing their domestic staff with them, have long gone. The lady on the right looks most uncertain about whether to go in after all.

'For 6d we occupied a bathing machine for half-an-hour. Each machine had a rope which we were supposed to hang on to regardless of whether we could swim or not. As the tide turned the machine was pulled up the shingle by a horse. The bathing woman yelled a warning, essential for the whole machine rocked from side to side. Goodness knows why there were no accidents.'

Above left: The latest swimwear fashions in 1900. 'Our bathing costumes were most decent. My mother's reached to her ankles with a skirt to her knees, with frills, and the long sleeves had frills at the wrist. My rather daring model ended at the elbows and knees.'

Above right: A advertisement for Gowland's, one of the many firms servicing bathing machines.

The rush to the sea: bathing machines enter the swirling waves just below the Wish Tower in the 1890s. 'A band played on the beach morning and afternoon for those who preferred not to risk their lives in them.'

The 'Birdcage' bandstand, Grand Parade, 1926. The Duke of Devonshire's Orchestra was subsumed into the Municipal Orchestra after the First World War. Captain Henry Amers, the orchestra conductor 1920–36, inaugurated an Annual Music Festival in 1923, the start of a fine tradition of orchestral and military band music. Always smartly attired, it was whispered that Amers wore a corset.

The 3,000-seat Central Bandstand, built at a cost of £29,000 to replace the Birdcage. It was officially opened on 5 August 1935 by Lord Leconfield. Over the years it has hosted many popular concerts, successfully continuing the tradition of military music. It is now a listed building but could do with more than a lick of paint.

The *James Stevens No.6* lifeboat in 1907. James Erridge is the coxswain. Bones Hide is third from right, with moustache. George John Erridge, third from left, went to St Valery in 1940 to bring home troops. The Terriss Memorial Lifeboat Station, seen behind the boat, was built by subscription after the murder of actor William Terriss (1847–97). It was in the wrong place – the lifeboat crew lived to the east – so it wasn't used after 1924 and on 22 March 1937 it became Britain's first Lifeboat Museum.

Looking east from near the Wish Tower over Grand Parade and bathing machines, *c.* 1900.

Above left: Johanna Maria (Jenny) Lind (1820-87), the 'Swedish Nightingale', occupied Cliff Cottage on two separate occasions around 1840. It was a one-storey stone building near today's Lascelles Terrace. She was frequently on the beach and was 'most affable'. Another holidaymaker was Alfred Lord Tennyson (1809-92); he stayed at Eastbourne in 1843, when he occupied Mount Pleasant, near the present Cavendish Hotel, and in 1845, when he stayed at No. 22 Seahouses, near the Albion Hotel.

Above right: William, seventh Duke of Devonshire (1808-91) was largely responsible for the orderly development of Eastbourne and played his part in the foundation of Eastbourne College.

Eastbournians showed their appreciation of the seventh Duke of Devonshire's 'worthy life' by erecting this statue by W. Goscombe John in Devonshire Place in 1901, the cost borne by voluntary subscriptions.

Tower 73, known as the Wish Tower, is Eastbourne's own Martello tower. The name 'Martello' comes from a fort in Corsica whose stout resistance impressed the Royal Navy. The Wish was the area of marshy ground that surrounded the greensand outcrop upon which the tower was built. Plans were drawn up in 1804 and the towers constructed between 1805 and 1812, 'to protect the exposed coast'; of those between Beachy Head and Pevensey only six remain. The Wish Tower was used for museums over the years but is troubled with damp. In the Second World War, two 6in guns were mounted in front.

The Wish Tower café and lounge was provided by Gilbert Foyle (1886-1971), of bookshop fame, in tribute to the town's fortitude during the war. He was a member of the council 1952-62.

The Wish Tower, c. 1895. On the left is Hounson's ticket office for bathing machine hire.

Edwardian cricket on the beach. The Alexandra Hotel in Grand Parade, centre, is almost unchanged today. The tower on the right was the house belonging to the manager of the Devonshire Park Baths, is now the Heritage Centre.

The Snoot Parade in 1905. This was the scene on a Sunday morning when visitors and local elites exhibited their finery, and the exquisitely finished belles and beaux eyed each other over. It also showed that you could afford an army of servants to prepare luncheon. The Grand Hotel is on the right; when it opened in 1877 it had six bathrooms for 200 bedrooms.

View from the first slopes of Beachy Head, *c.* 1935. The nearest house is Holywell Mount, where one of Dr Bodkin Adams' patients died. Behind are St Bede's School, the West Parades and Helen Garden, given by Mrs Helen Hornsby Lewis, an ICI millionaire, who lived in South Cliff.

Holywell in the 1960s. This area had been the Gore Chalk Pit, from which chalk was exported by sea. In 1904, as part of scheme to reduce seasonal unemployment, it was laid out as gardens at a cost of £400, which the borough had to borrow. Further work followed in the 1920s.

Upper Duke's Drive, c. 1892. The seventh Duke financed a massive series of works to landscape the Eastbourne front and use the chalk spoil to build up roads and foundations in the town. At the western end of the parades, he built this wonderfully curving entrance to the town from Beachy Head. It is no longer possible to see the view, due mainly to the growth of vegetation.

Looking back eastwards over Meads from the first slopes of the Downs, c. 1895. On the left in the middle distance is All Saints Convalescent Hospital and, in the centre, St Luke's Children's Convalescent Hospital (now Dolphin Court flats). In the days when recovery from broken bones or pneumonia took months, any resort boasting health-giving properties had to have convalescent hospitals.

Holywell Promenade, at the west end of the front, c. 1900. The thatched chalet is a feature to this day. A fine parade of bath chairs is on show.

Eastbourne front from Foyle Way and the pinnacle in the west, looking past the Parades to the Wish Tower and the pier. South Cliff Tower can be seen on the left; it is a desirable residence in a lovely part of the town, but considered most intrusive and 'not Eastbourne' by most people.

King George V and Queen Mary visit Eastbourne in March 1935, before the exertions of their Silver Jubilee celebrations. They rested at Chalet No. 2 at Holywell, which has a plaque recording the event. It is rumoured that the King was displeased by the excessive attention accorded to the visit and so didn't bestow the handle 'Regis' on the town.

The boldest, most romantic and highest chalk foreland on the South Coast, and the most dangerous. Around 100 million years ago, when dinosaurs ruled the earth, it was formed under the sea from the skeletons of myriads of small sea creatures, taking some 15 million years. Later it was lifted up out of the sea by rock movements. The Normans called it Beauchef, 'Beautiful Headland', a name corrupted to Beachy Head. The 160m (535ft) foreland majestically protects Eastbourne from the south–west gales, earning the town the name 'The Suntrap of the South'.

Beachy Head is known all over the world. A battle and a racehorse have been named after it, and it is featured on hundreds of postcards. It appears in the phrase 'Birmingham by way of Beachy Head', meaning a tortuous route. Perhaps the greatest accolade was when it became the subject for a 1936 Senior Service cigarette card. Artists have pictured it in all its ways, such as this icy view by Edward Lear (1812-88), a regular visitor to the town, who complained of the distance he had to walk to get there.

Beachy Head, c. 1910. On the left is the Beachy Head Hotel. The Coastguard Cottages, centre, were damaged in the Second World War and knocked down in 1950 to build an underground nuclear bunker. On the right is the Watch Tower with its semaphore signalling mast; it was run by Lloyds to observe shipping for the London insurance and commodity markets and is now an observation platform owned by the town.

One of the steam locomotives named after Beachy Head, Atlantic H2-class No. 32424, built in 1911 and destroyed in 1958. It is shown in the sidings at Brighton on 31 August 1957.

Beachy Head was featured in the Royal Mail's Safety at Sea series issued on 18 June 1985.

The Beachy Head Hotel, *c.* 1930. A few bombs dropped on Beachy Head during the Second World War, including incendiaries, but the hotel survived until 1966, when it burnt down. At the time, it had no mains water supply and a strong wind fanned the flames. It was rebuilt but burnt down again in 1994. However, Whitbread's got it going again within the year as a Brewer's Fayre.

Above left: Rupert Brooke (1887-1915), poet and icon of his age, made several visits to Eastbourne and stayed at the Beachy Head Hotel in 1911. Perhaps he asked, 'And is there honey still for tea?' Like so many of his generation, Brooke was to perish in the First World War; he died on the way to the Dardanelles from an infected insect bite.

Above right: The Duchess of York, later the Queen Mother, when she visited Eastbourne on 29 October 1929 to commemorate the Downs Purchase.

This was the guardhouse for the Cold War nuclear bunker. After 1957 it housed the coastguard rescue gear and stabled the police horse in the 1960s and '70s. It was knocked down in the 1990s as part of an environmental clean-up.

Signalman's Cottage on Beachy Head, built by Lloyds of London for their watchkeeper, was situated just west of the hotel. After 1904, when ship telegraphy came in, it was used as tea rooms and as a Natural History Centre. Torched in 1992, all evidence of its existence has been completely erased.

On 29 October 1929 the Duke and Duchess of York (later King George VI and Queen Elizabeth) unveiled commemorative tablets on this seat, recording the Beachy Head Downs Purchase by Eastbourne County Borough. The seat was damaged in the Second World War and replaced in 1979 by seats more in keeping with the surroundings than this ornate creation.

PC Jack Williams on Jumbo, a 17½-hands dappled grey, *c.* 1970. There was a mounted police Downs Ranger from 1929, when the borough purchased the Downs. PC Henry Poole, whose best loved horse was Princess Patricia, patrolled to 1953, when PC Harry Ward took over Poole was involved in many rescues and recoveries of those who had fallen over the cliffs.

The coastguard station and Coastguard Cottages on Beachy Head, built in the 1870s. They were damaged in the Second World War but remained in use throughout; they were only demolished for the nuclear bunker in 1950. The bunker, 75m (250ft) long, is said to be like putting the equivalent of the Grand Hotel underground.

Above left: The Beachy Head ex-Lloyds Watch Tower, with the semaphore mast; you can still find where some of the guy ropes were stayed. It became a postcard kiosk and, after being damaged in the Second World War, was given to the council, who made it into an observation platform with a telescope.

Above right: The *Royal Sovereign* lightship, *c.* 1910. It was replaced by the 1971 Light Tower, situated around 10 miles out to sea, right where the Battle of Beachy Head was fought in 1690.

Over his 10 years as Downs Ranger, from 1953-63, PC Harry Ward designed a lightweight stretcher for rescues. As the beach is stony and not suited to carrying a stretcher for any distance, he used this winch apparatus to bring the victim back up the cliff. It needed three men to lift it, however, and had only two speeds: slow and imperceptible.

During a 1964 police parade at Beachy Head, the Duke of Norfolk presented the British Empire Medal to PC Harry Ward for his bravery when helping those who had fallen over the cliff and for developing improved equipment in order to provide a faster and safer response.

In 1973 the coastguard took over the recovery and rescue of cliff-fall victims. For this August 1988 rescue, the coastguard-in-charge, Garry Russell, guides the rescueman (in crash helmet) and assistants as they use a light derrick that Garry had designed to bring the stretcher-wrapped victim up to the cliff top. A capstan attached to a Land Rover pays out the lines. Using this system, the rescueman could be lowered to the bottom within 5 minutes.

Nowadays, a helicopter is often used to convey victims to safety as soon and as comfortably as possible. Here, three students cut off by the high tide are rescued by helicopter. Sometimes one of the lifeboats comes inshore to help.

Above: Innumerable shipwrecks have occurred at Beachy Head. The Venetians called it Caput Doble, 'the Devil's Headland', with its jagged submerged rocks running out for half a mile and its capricious winds. The earliest known wrecking was the *Marie* of Santander in 1368 but most went unrecorded. In 1747, when the Spanish *Nympha Americana* ran ashore and broke up, spilling precious metals and fine raiments, crowds of people came and carried off what they could of the cargo.

Left: Darby's Cave in 1899. Jonathan Darby, vicar of nearby East Dean 1705-26, was so distressed by the number of seamen washed ashore each winter that he determined to reduce the toll himself. So he opened up smugglers' caves near Belle Tout, where he would repair during stormy nights to display a warning light over long watches, which must have been cold and wet. As is inscribed on his gravestone in East Dean church, 'He was the Sailors' Friend'.

A 1691 petition to Trinity House for a lighthouse at Beachy Head went unheeded and a lighthouse wasn't built until 1828, after an East Indiaman, the *Thames*, hit rocks off the headland and ran ashore at Eastbourne in 1822. It was the subject of many paintings and, with publicity in the press adding to the agitation, in 1828 'Mad' Jack Fuller, MP and folly builder, built a wooden lighthouse at Belle Tout, a point on the cliffs around 85m (285ft) high with good all-round views. In 1834 Trinity House replaced it with a lighthouse of Aberdeen granite (brought from Maidstone on ox carts). On a clear night, the light could be seen 23 miles out to sea, and local guides included it in their itineraries.

The Belle Tout lighthouse, 1874. The name 'Belle Tout' is not French, but comes from the Celtic god Bael and the Saxon word 'toot', meaning a lookout. There is a bit of artistic licence in this picture, as the artist has the sea on the landward side. Sadly, the lighthouse was not a success as a warning light, for on dark, misty nights, just when a sailor needed a guide, the light shone uselessly over the mist and the wrecks continued, including two at the cliffs right underneath.

Above left: The Belle Tout lighthouse after it was decommissioned in 1902. In 1923 it was bought by the distinguished neurologist Sir James Purves Stewart for £1,500; he had lived in Eastbourne as a lad.

Above right: Sir James installed a generator, an access road, added another storey and entertained King George V and Queen Mary there in March 1935.

It was a different scene in 1945 after Belle Tout had been ravaged by friendly fire in 1942. Sir James donated it to the borough of Eastbourne in 1948, after pocketing £5,000 in war compensation. The borough leased it to Dr E.R. Cullinan in 1956 and he had made it sound by 1960. The cliffs to the left are the Seven Sisters.

Belle Tout was used as the £¼ million set of the 1986 BBC TV series *The Life and Loves of a She Devil* with Patricia Hodge and Dennis Waterman. All the landscaped gardens soon blew down but the ex-lighthouse was finally restored.

A massive cliff fall in January 1999 stretched almost to the Beachy Head lighthouse. The chalk erodes at a rate of 0.5m (18in) a year and Belle Tout (just visible) was about to be in danger.

Above: Belle Tout, 1997. Parts of the lighthouse were less than 5m from the edge, compared with over 40m in 1834. It was decided to attempt a £250,000 operation to slide it back.

Right: Starting on 17 March 1999, the tower and living quarters were moved back 17m (50ft) on greased runners for another 25 years of life, at a cost of £15,000 per metre. Glass flower vases and other delicate items were quite safe on shelves all through the move.

The move was an international event, with coverage from the world's media and thousands watching. It moved at a rate of 1m every 40 minutes, including breaks to reposition the jacks, a hardly perceptible rate. This photograph was taken about halfway through the operation.

The Belle Tout lighthouse, which has survived into the twenty-first century. The little gate in the wall (centre) was level with the rear window of the living quarters before the move.

Above: Between 1899 and 1902, Trinity House embarked on an ambitious project to build Beachy Head lighthouse at the foot of the cliffs. All the workmen, materials and equipment travelled down by a cable running from the top of the cliff to a work platform on site above the high-water mark. The foundations were sunk 5m into the chalk and 3,600 tons of Cornish granite went on top. The new lighthouse was nearly 140ft (40m) high, and cost £20,814.

Right: The ligthouse nearing completion. The 720 Cornish granite blocks were shaped at the quarry. The light came into operation on 2 October 1902, the Hood vaporiser being fuelled with a distillate similar to paraffin oil. It shows two white flashes – which can be seen 16 miles out to sea in almost all conditions – every 20 seconds and the foghorn gives one blast every 30 seconds.

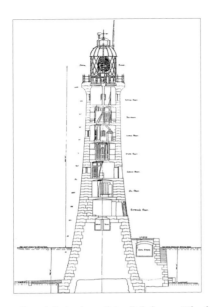

Above left: A plan of the lighthouse. The lamp is over 30m (103ft) above the average sea level. Before electrification in 1974, it had to be trimmed every day and oil pumped up from a tank near the base. The service room was below the lamp room, then the bedroom for three resident lighthousemen, and below was their living room. Down further were storerooms, the crane room, the oil room and the entrance area. A spiral staircase connected the top to the bottom, where 'the heads' (the toilets) were to be found! The lighthouse was automated in 1983.

Above right: The size of the lighthouse is only appreciated from the beach, for it seems like a toy when seen from the top of Beachy Head

In spite of all its turbulent history and reputation, Beachy Head is a delightful spot for a stroll; the soft Downland turf, the fresh sea breezes and the views are a delight to body and mind. On Easter Monday 1987 the mayor, Leslie Mason, and the mayoress opened a Peace Path to celebrate the UN Year of Peace and to provide improved access for the disabled to Beachy Head's delights.

two

Aviation

Left: Gustav Hamel (1889–1914), of immortal fame in aircraft history, with a Blériot monoplane in Eastbourne in 1913. Hamel knew the Eastbourne airfield well and often performed a loop-the-loop to delight the crowds, once in brilliant moonlight over the pier. When he landed, he remarked that he had enjoyed seeing the lights of France from Eastbourne during the manoeuvre.

Above right: Bernard Fowler (1883–1967) and his wife Josephine setting off on their honeymoon on 11 October 1913. Fired by Blériot's cross-Channel flight in 1909, Fowler formed the Eastbourne Aviation Co. (EAC) in 1911, with an airfield near St Anthony's Hill and a seaplane base by today's Sovereign Centre. Apart from designing four aircraft, none of which 'got off the ground', the EAC taught nineteen men to fly before 1914, most of whom served in the First World War.

Workers at the EAC during the First World War. The factory was erected near where the Sovereign Centre stands today. In the course of the war, 252 aircraft were assembled by the EAC. Work ceased there in 1924. Some buildings were sold to the council and were used to stack deckchairs. One hangar by Leeds Avenue was used during the Second World War; it was later used as a furniture repository and finally as a bus museum, until it was demolished in 1991 after being damaged in the 1987 'hurricane'.

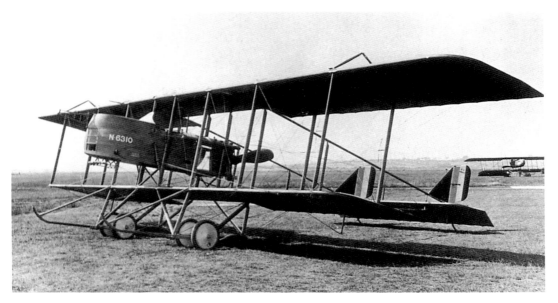

An Eastbourne-assembled Maurice Farman Shorthorn 'pusher' biplane N6310 in July 1917.

The crew of airship SSZ39, A.M. Brock DFM, Lt W.E. Bryan DFC and A.M. Wilkins, established a flight duration record when they flew for 50 hours 55 minutes during an anti-submarine patrol over the Channel. From 1915-18 there was an Royal Naval Air Service (later RAF) airship station at Polegate. The site ran in a north-westerly direction from near the Willingdon triangle along Coppice Avenue. The only real disaster involving loss of life was in December 1917, when in bad weather an airship that had lost its way collided with one that had made an emergency landing near Jevington.

An Avro 504L seaplane used for joyrides along the Eastbourne seafront in 1919-20. After the First World War, Fowler tried every ruse to make the EAC successful, including joyrides, aerial photography and a School of Flying for Ladies. He even used his planes to guide hunts to their quarry, but to no avail. After the company went bust, Fowler was sent to Japan for a year as part of an official mission to teach the Japanese, who had been allies in the First World War, to fly.

Herbert George Wells (1866-1946), inventive author of works such as *The War of the Worlds* (1898) and *The Time Machine* (1895). Wells took holidays in Eastbourne and had his first flight from the beach. He wrote an introduction to George Meek's *Bath-chairman by Himself*, a story about the hard, unrewarding graft of pulling a bath chair along Eastbourne's glorious front.

Pioneer aviatrix Amy Johnson landed her plane, the bottle-green DH60 Gipsy Moth *Jason*, at Frowds Field along Kings Drive, Eastbourne, in 1930. She set up many flying records and was the darling of the nation. She died ferrying planes in the war, probably shot down by friendly fire. Her fiancé Jim Mollison force-landed his Gipsy Moth at Pevensey on 6 August 1931. The crowd that gathered cut a hedge down to give him a longer run so that he could take off again; he landed later that day at Croydon aerodrome, having flown from Australia in 8 days and 22 hours.

With ominous black clouds gathering amid fears of another world war, Gordon Clark said, 'On 2 July 1931, I saw the Graf Zeppelin pass along the coast. The silvery cigar was enormous, it seemed to fill the sky. People said they knew why it came – to take photographs of our naval installations, and they were probably right.'

An Me 109 landed beside the A259 at Eastbourne in September 1940. The engine was misfiring beforehand – witnesses thought the pilot was shooting at them – as a result of a coolant leak. The intrepid members of the Home Guard seen here are Don Dann and Derrick Pyle. The pilot, Horst Perez, was taken by PC Harry Hyde to the police house, where he was given a cup of tea. The almost untouched plane had an exciting second career: it was sent to Canada as part of a drive to raise dollars for the war effort and then went to the US, where it was exhibited at numerous cities and for extra donations people could sign their names on it. It returned to Canada, where it rested for decades, until it came back to the UK and was restored. It is now at Duxford Aircraft Museum as the only surviving German plane to take part in the Battle of Britain.

This Me 109 crash-landed near Black Robin Farm in June 1942 after being hit by anti-aircraft fire while strafing shipping and installations on Beachy Head. The farmer's wife, Eileen Goldsmith, saw the 22-year-old pilot being led away and remarked, 'He only looked 18 to me'.

Aircrew in front of their plane at Friston Advanced Landing Ground, 1944. It was primarily designed so that damaged planes, unable to make their base, could belly-flop as soon as they reached the coast. Some seventy-eight planes force-landed during January 1944. Lysanders also took off on Special Operations Executive missions and Spitfires flew from here to discourage the 'hit-and-run' raids of 1942-43.

A Slingsby 21B glider is launched by winch from the old Friston Advanced Landing Ground, just west of Eastbourne. There was a gliding club here between 1946 and 1955. The club moved their hangar from Portslade, where it had been before the war. With Air Vice Marshal Sir John Salmond as president, the membership of the club reached around seventy. Ray Brigden says, 'It was an eminently suitable site for gliders, the only disadvantage was that the grazing cattle didn't always co-operate'. The club moved to Firle in March 1955.

On Saturday 4 June 1955, the Duke of Edinburgh came to Eastbourne for the silver jubilee of the Royal Air Forces Association. A Short Sunderland Mk V flying boat, coming in for an air show, misjudged the landing and sank just off the beach. Sadly, one airman was killed and three injured.

The Utterly Butterly wing walkers show their paces at *Airbourne* 2004. The *Airbourne* air show has been held annually along the front since the 1990s. The Red Arrows usually appear and there is also a car exhibition, and 250,000 people pour into the town for the show. The air show is continuing the town's association with aviation, which has existed since 1909.

three

Businesses
and Shops

Above left: You find the name of Ebenezer Morris's ironworks on most of the lamp-posts, gutters, manhole covers, railings and (as above) coal-hole covers installed in Eastbourne between 1850 and 1910.

Above right: Henry Evenden (1833-93) set up shop in the 1850s with John Terry (1830-70) as draper and silk merchant in what is now Memorial Square.

One of the first locals to achieve success was Henry Sutton. From a shoemaking family, he branched out in 1861 as manager of the Railway Hotel (now a NatWest bank) on the corner of Terminus Road and Cornfield Road. With the building of Upperton Road, the Gilbert Arms (known as the Squirrel from the Davies-Gilbert crest) had to be demolished and Sutton acquired a plot near the station and built the Gildredge Hotel, to which the Gilbert Arms licence was transferred in 1870. An astute businessman, he became a Freemason and an alderman, with a farm at Horam. The Gildredge Hotel was bombed in 1940.

STAR BREWERY.

ALEX. HURST & CO.,

Brewers, AND Maltsters,

WINE & SPIRIT IMPORTERS,

EASTBOURNE.

BREWERY AND OFFICES:—
OLD TOWN.

BRANCH OFFICES AND STORES:—
64c, TERMINUS ROAD.

Families supplied with India Pale Ale, Bitter Beer and Nourishing Stout, in small Casks or Bottle.

PRICE LISTS MAY BE HAD ON APPLICATION.

ESTABLISHED 1777.

William Hurst founded the Old Town Brewery in 1777 and it lasted as the Star Brewery into the 1960s. Now the site is occupied by houses, flats and a supermarket.

Caleb Diplock's off-licence in Terminus Road is now the Portman Building Society; however, the fabric has hardly changed. Caleb Diplock's Lion Steam Brewery was perhaps Eastbourne's most successful business venture. Diplock came to the town in 1856 and bought a house in Terminus Road, calling it London House. In 1858 he bought the Commercial Hotel (Diplock's Hotel) and in 1863 his brewery and malthouse opened. By 1883 Caleb had sold up and retired with 'a noble fortune', but he died the next year. When his son died in 1936 at the age of ninety-five, he left £½ million and a load of trouble. The will was contested, a lawyer died tragically, and the House of Lords ruled it void. The matter wasn't settled for fourteen years.

Above: Louis G. Ford's ironmongery in Station Parade, 1960s. Ford made his first sale, 5s (25p), at his shop in the newly built parade in January 1912. Alongside were coal merchants Rickett's and Bradford's; they had been on the site for some time in one-storey station huts. By the 1960s, Ford's (now Graham's) had taken over the whole parade. Also in 1912, the head post office was built opposite, at No. 3 Upperton Road, and Bobby & Co. completed their Lismore Road store (now Debenhams).

Right: In 1856 William Morris Caffyn was apprenticed to his uncle Ebenezer Morris to learn the trade of 'ironmonger, tinman and brazier' at 2s (10p) a week. He opened his first shop on 19 May 1865, at the far end of this row in Meads Road, as a gas and hot water fitter.

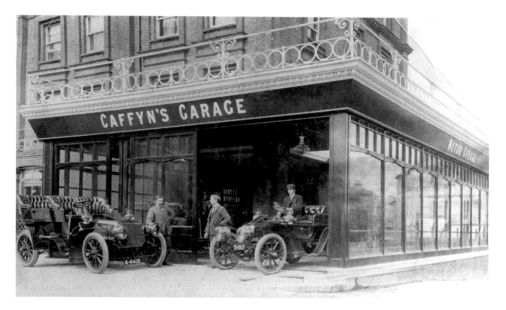

Caffyn's Garage, Marine Parade, 1904. William's sons, Percy and Harry, decided that the future lay in cars and they opened the garage in 1902. The first motor car was seen on Eastbourne's roads in May 1896; Caffyn's alone were selling over 1,000 cars a year by 1929.

Opposite below: The first Marks & Spencer shop in Eastbourne opened on 27 July 1912 at No. 51 Terminus Road. In those days, you were expected to buy something if you entered a shop, which is why there is an 'Admission Free' sign above the door. Marks & Spencer extended the shop to include No. 53 in 1937, but it was flattened in the terrible Christmas bombing of 1942, when over fifty women and children were killed or injured. Temporary premises were used until the shop reopened in May 1955 at the old site (now Nos 133–137 Terminus Road).

Caffyn's Garage was completely destroyed in a direct hit by a 500kg bomb on 6 June 1943. The site is now a roundabout.

Caffyn's opened their new office and workshops in Upperton Road in 1965, a century after William Caffyn started the business. By that time, the business was in the competent hands of his grandchildren, with a turnover of more than £10 million and a staff of 1,500. A 1930s publicity booklet stated that 'Caffyn's will only act as agents for British cars – they are not prepared to push the sale of foreign cars'. This romance with British marques lasted until 1977, when the company acquired the Fiat and Mercedes franchises. Caffyn's took over an old established car firm, Clark & Lambert, at around the same time and are now agents for many manufacturers, including Volkswagen; they bought Skinner's, the Volkswagen dealers, in 2002.

A bird's-eye view of the Birds Eye factory in Lottbridge Drove around 1975. It was the largest factory on the estate, profitably turning out millions of frozen food products, but a rationalisation determined its closure, which commenced in 1983.

A frozen-cake production line at Birds Eye, c. 1975. It wasn't the first big factory in Eastbourne – that was Armour Pharmaceuticals in 1954 – but it was the largest. The site is now occupied by a Tesco superstore, which moved from the Langney shopping centre, Eastbourne's first.

Tavistock, a block of luxury flats in Eastbourne built by Walter Llewellyn & Sons. Walter and William Llewellyn started as jobbing builders in 1899 and went from strength to strength. The firm celebrated its centenary with a £140 million turnover, but was taken over by ROK in 2002.

One of the regular 25 Club luncheons that Walter Llewellyn & Sons gave for all employees who had clocked up 25 years of service.

four

Law and
Some
Disorder

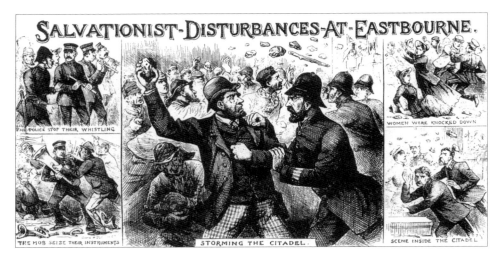

The Salvation Army came to Eastbourne in 1890 and opened their citadel in Langney Road. The organisation was welcome but there was irritation when their band broke the 1885 Eastbourne Improvement Act by marching and playing on a Sunday. The main antipathy, however, was to 'furriners' coming into the county. Skirmishes broke out and there were attempts to stop the Salvation Army band by the 'Skeleton Army', probably lager louts encouraged by publicans worried over the possibility of stricter licensing laws, although the mayor was also opposed. One result of the disturbances was that in 1891 Eastbourne formed its own police force, splitting from the Sussex County Police.

The Salvation Army band play peacefully on the beach near the Burlington Hotel in 1898. The culmination of the opposition to their Sunday playing came on 19 July 1891, with the arrest of members of the Camberwell band, who had come to lend encouragement. In 1892, the Salvation Army promoted a Parliamentary Bill to change the law and the episode passed.

Eastbourne 20 Nov 1835

Dear Sir,

I regret to inform you that we have had, and still have, a great disturbance in the Eastbourne Workhouse. The married persons in this house appear to have conspired to prevent the separation of man and wife. All the married women took advantage of the occasion of cleaning out the men's apartments and went to their husbands and they all resolutely refused to be again separated ... The conduct of the parties has been most desperate: fortunately it happened to be the Board day, and the Guardians have (by force) succeeded in getting two of the worst characters (men) into the blackhole. Some have been prevailed upon to be again separated, but the house still continues in great confusion. The Governor is protected for the night by the constables and headboroughs and a Special

The Grand Parade Murder of 1860

Elizabeth Brockhurst

Eastbourne Local History Society

Above: The first recorded disturbance in Eastbourne was a protest over the policy of separating husbands and wives in the new workhouse in 1835: 'All the married women took advantage of the occasion of cleaning out the men's apartments and went to their husbands and they all resolutely refused to be separated. The conduct of the parties has been most desperate ... the house still continues in great confusion.'

Left: Thomas Hopley set up a school at No. 22 Grand Parade for the sons of gentlemen. On 21 April 1860 Reginald Cancellor, 14, was called to Hopley's study following 'intransigence' and beaten for two hours. The next morning the boy was found dead, but the inquest verdict was 'natural causes'. The boy's brother came to Eastbourne, saw bruises on the body and demanded a post mortem; when this showed horrifying injuries, Hopley was arrested, charged with manslaughter, found guilty and sentenced to four years. At the trial, the Lord Chief Justice laid down that any parent or schoolmaster had a right to beat a boy, but in moderation and never in anger. Amazingly, there were people who thought Hopley had suffered 'a most remarkable injustice'.

On 6 October 1912 a cabman saw a figure crouching on the canopy above the door of No. 6 South Cliff Avenue (on the right). Inspector Walls attended the scene and went up to the man, saying, 'Come down, old chap, do'. The burglar shot Walls, who staggered into the street, where he shortly died. A sordid story was revealed of a burglar who went under many aliases, John Williams being on the charge sheet. The event had a tremendous effect in the town – 'Is nowhere safe?' – and thousands attended the inspector's funeral. Williams was tried, found guilty, and hanged the next year.

In 1918 scandalous wrongdoings were again associated with No. 22 Grand Parade. When Georges Hayes, of that address and manager of the pier, was called up for the armed forces, he attempted to obtain the birth certificate of another George Hayes, aged 51, and sent a Winifred Houghton to Liverpool with this intent. He was apprehended, and at his trial in May, he was found guilty. Major Edward Teale, Eastbourne's chief constable, spoke for him and the sentence was only three months. At this time, evading call-up was considered the most heinous conduct and there was such an uproar that an enquiry was instituted into the chief constable's conduct. It became clear that there had been an improper attempt to influence the court and Major Teale was forced to resign, although he managed to walk away with a pension of £170 a year.

EASTBOURNE CHRONICLE,

A REMARKABLE CASE.

DEVICE TO ESCAPE MILITARY SERVICE.

In consequence of an illegal attempt to evade liability for military service, Mr. George Hayes, aged 43, secretary and manager to the Eastbourne Pier Company, has been sentenced by the Liverpool Stipendiary to two separate terms of six weeks' imprisonment in the second division. The case came up on Tuesday, when Hayes was charged with having conspired with Winifred Gertrude Houghton (30), also of Eastbourne, to obtain the birth certificate of one George Hayes, boilermaker, Vinmore-street, Liverpool, with a view to so using the same that he would escape being called up for military duty. A plea of guilty was tendered, and the woman Houghton confessed to having wilfully acted as the male defendant's agent. There was a further charge against both defendants (also admitted) of having given false information on a Liverpool hotel registration form.

Mr. Cripps, who prosecuted, said Hayes had instructed the female to obtain the birth certificate of "some other George Hayes," but above the military age," the intention being to use such certificate as a means of evading military service. In furtherance of this device he sent the woman to Liverpool, she being told to there search the directory for the

TOW

57, TER

Messrs. Town Houses in Ea fully Selected

HIGH PO Reside rooms, bath r 8 guineas per

CENTRAL and sho bedrooms, ba 7 guineas per

MEADS. Detach aspect, compr room, lavator rooms, smoke separate stai dressing roo bottom and f electric light and linen co rent 16 guinea

HIGH PO Reside bedrooms, ba

Irene Munro, 17, was the victim of the first grisly murder on the Crumbles, labelled 'The Seance on the Shingle'. She came to Eastbourne for her holidays and on 19 August 1920 she was seen on the Crumbles 'happy and laughing in the company of two men'. Later that day her body was found battered to death. Descriptions of the men were obtained and Jack Field, 19, and William Gray, 28, both unemployed, were apprehended on the seafront. There was little doubt of their guilt, although each claimed the other had struck the fatal blow, and both were executed the next year.

Patrick Mahon (with a coat over his head) is brought back to the scene of his murder of Emily Kaye in 1924. Dr (later Sir) Bernard Spilsbury, the forensic pathologist, thought that Eastbourne's second murder on the Crumbles was his most interesting case. Mahon, 34, a persistent philanderer with a record of embezzlement and violent robbery, struck up a relationship with Kaye, 37. She found herself pregnant, and told her friends she was going away with 'Pat'. Scotland Yard, having been tipped off by Mahon's wife, arrested Mahon and he admitted that he had been to Eastbourne with Emily. In a rented cottage, police found a trunk, with the initials EBK, which held human body parts. Spilsbury reassembled them, showing that they were of a pregnant woman. At the trial, Spilsbury proved that Kaye didn't die by falling, as claimed by Mahon. Mahon convicted himself by stating that he bought a knife after Kaye's death, as the police had the bill dated from before the murder. He was hanged at Wandsworth.

Eastbourne Gazette

NO. 3595   SEVENTY-SECOND YEAR OF PUBLICATION   WEDNESDAY, APRIL 5, 1933   REGISTERED AT THE G.P.O. AS A NEWSPAPER   PRICE TWOPENCE

BRIBERY AND CORRUPTION CHARGES

ELECTRICAL CONTRACTS PROSECUTION

EX-ALDERMAN AND OFFICIAL BEFORE THE MAGISTRATES

PUBLIC PROSECUTOR'S CASE AT YESTERDAY'S HEARING

THE FUN FAIR

"WE HATE THE THING," SAY ENGINEERS

GIRL'S DESIRE FOR ADVENTURE

FOUND AT EASTBOURNE AFTER MISSING FROM HOME

LAD WITH DAGGER AND REVOLVER

LENIENT COURSE TAKEN AT QUARTER SESSIONS

At the end of 1931 Pirelli's made a claim against Eastbourne Corporation in respect of electrical contracts. Bribery was discovered and in April 1933 Pirelli's, Richard Chatfield, now an ex-alderman, David Roberts, ex-Deputy Borough Electrical Engineer, and Mr Reed, an official of Pirelli's, pleaded guilty to various charges. Chatfield and Roberts were each fined £250, Reed £50 and Pirelli's £550.

Above left: A dinner card for a police function in March 1936 at the Town Hall. The card's design is a reference to the introduction of driving tests and Belisha beacons the previous year.

Above right: The Eastbourne contingent for the Coronation inspection by HM The Queen at Hyde Park in 1953. The men are standing on the steps of the main police station in Grove Road.

Eastbourne County Borough Police, 1938. Commander W.H. Smith is seated centre front. Eastbourne's first policeman wasn't appointed by the Sussex County Police until 1842. The police performed tremendous work during the Second World War, assisting bombed-out families and helping to keep the systems running through blackouts and air raids.

Dr John Bodkin Adams (1899-1983), stands second from right at a function with Norah O'Hara (sitting second from left), to whom he was engaged at one time. Adams was a local GP who in 1956-57 was accused of the murder of three patients – the press said 400. The dramatic moments of his murder trial and the publicity over the case influenced the introduction in 1967 of reporting restrictions in court, and set a case law that treatment inadvertently causing death was not murder. Speculation continues to this day as to whether he was a murderer or a disorganised caring doctor. Eastbourne had another dramatic white-collar crime in 1995, when Graham Durnford Ford, a solicitor, was found guilty of fraud and sentenced to ten years' imprisonment. The Law Society's Compensation Fund had to pay out £9 million in its largest claim to date.

Views of the 62m high South Cliff Tower. The tale of Eastbourne's carbuncle began in 1960 when Mayor Katie Juliette Underhay put plans before the council to pull down Hillcote, a school on South Cliff, and replace it with a block of high-class flats. A storm of protest followed but in 1966 South Cliff Tower was completed. There was a surge of revulsion and a determination that nothing like 'Katie's Folly' should happen again. One result was that Underhay was thrown off the council by the voters.

Mayor Underhay, receiving the guests at an official reception in 1966.

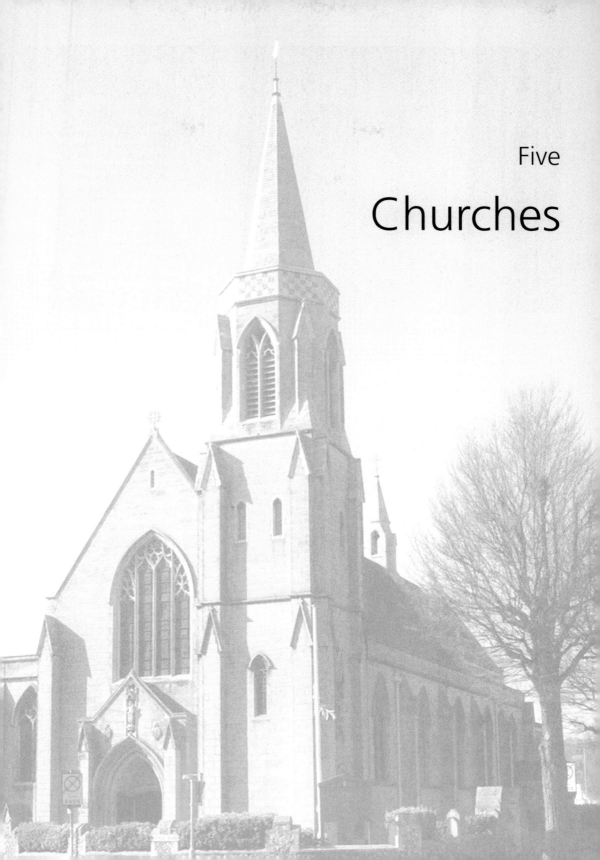

Five

Churches

St Mary's parish church, around 1875, the only church in the town until 1810. This medieval church dates from 1160, was extended in the 1300s and restored in Victorian times. It is built of Caen stone, chequered flints and greensand and contains tablet brasses to John King 1445 and James Graves 1647. The chancel, unusually, is below the nave level. The central east window is in Early Decorated style, as are the fine oak screens. The north aisle windows, the font and tower are in Perpendicular style.

Holy Trinity church was built in 1838 to cater for the increasing number of residents living near the seafront. The Earl of Burlington (later the seventh Duke of Devonshire) provided the site and the Revd Thomas Pitman, vicar of Eastbourne, raised the money by subscriptions. Originally designed by Decimus Burton, it became a parish church in 1847. It has since been substantially altered and enlarged, and had all but one of its windows blown out during the Blitz.

Christ Church, known as the fisherman's church, was designed by a Pugin associate, Benjamin Ferrey, and opened in 1859 on land given by the Davies-Gilbert family. It has a Willis organ. Princess Alice was a worshipper during her 1878 visit, and has a memorial window. The Revd Charles Dodgson (Lewis Carroll) preached here in 1893. Alongside is Brodie Hall Infants' School.

The foundation stone of St Saviour's church was laid in a turnip field donated by the Duke of Devonshire on 17 October 1865. Designed by G.E. Street in Gothic style and well built, as usual, by James Peerless, it was described by Goodheart-Rendel as 'a noble church'. It is the finest Victorian church in the town and, with its graceful broach spire, the loftiest at 55m (175ft). It has always been High Church; Emmanuel church (now the WRVS centre) was built 'in reaction to its incense-burning'.

St Peter's church stood on the corner of Meads and Granville Roads. It began as a chapel of ease for St Saviour's on a site behind the Town Hall in 1878. In 1894 this church, designed by Henry Currey, was erected. Although a listed building, it was declared redundant and knocked down in 1971-72. Redman King House now stands on the site.

All Souls church, with its Italianate Romanesque style, 83ft (25m) campanile and interior Byzantine capitals with walls of decorative banding, is one of the most striking churches in Sussex. Designed by A.P. Strong and erected in 1882, it was paid for by Lady Victoria Wellesley, a great-niece of the first Duke of Wellington and a resident of the town. Built on shifting 'beach', it is said there is more below ground than above.

The interior of the All Saints Convalescent Hospital Chapel in Meads. Designed in Gothic Revival style by Henry Woodyer, a follower of Butterfield, it was consecrated on 4 July 1874 by the Bishop of Chichester. Especially notable are the polychromatic effects of brick and stone, the fine geometric tiling, the tribune supported on marble columns and the Hardman stained glass. It is now Grade II★ listed. However, the hospital closed in 2004 and there is concern about the future of the chapel.

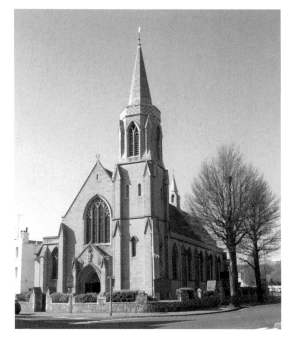

The foundation stone of Our Lady of Ransom church in Grange Road was laid on 11 December 1900. Built by Mark Martin to a Late Decorated Gothic style by F.A. Walters, in Bath stone (which doesn't relish salty winds), the church was opened on 15 December 1901 by Father Lynch in the presence of Bishop Bourne. By custom, it was not consecrated until 8 July 1926, when all debt had been settled. A tower was added in 1912 and a chancel and side chapels in 1920. Recently, a hall was also added. The church has also been listed.

When recluse Eliza Watson died, she left over £100,000 for the building of a church in Eastbourne. The town had too many churches in 1930 and the Bishop of Chichester wanted the money to build two or three churches in Brighton. However, the solicitor said the church had to be in Eastbourne and so a new parish was carved out and the massive St Elisabeth's church, with a palatial vicarage (to the right) and a grand church hall (to the left), duly constructed. The church was never satisfactory, with damp rapidly appearing, and it was damaged by flying bombs during the Second World War.

In 1944 the Bishop of Chichester asked Hans Feibusch to paint murals based on scenes from John Bunyan's *The Pilgrim's Progress* in the crypt of St Elisabeth's church. There was no hope for the church: the Parochial Church Council wanted to demolish and rebuild but the War Damage Commission said that they could only repair. It was repaired but bits continued to fall off and in 2004 it was decided to close the church and convert the hall into a place of worship.

six

Medicine and Hospitals

Right: Princess Alice (1843-78), the third child of Queen Victoria, came on holiday to Eastbourne in the autumn of 1878. She impressed the locals with her kindly nature and willingness to get involved in opening fêtes and other charity functions. Unfortunately, during her stay, the excursion paddle steamer *Princess Alice* collided with a collier and sank in 5 minutes, with the loss of 600 lives – the greatest peacetime disaster on the River Thames. Princess Alice had married the Grand Duke of Hesse and, shortly after her return to Germany, her children caught diphtheria and Alice and one of the children died. The people of Eastbourne were so shocked that they resolved to perpetuate her memory with a hospital. Princess Christian paid the first official royal visit to Eastbourne in 1882 to lay the foundation stone.

THE GRAPHIC

AN ILLUSTRATED WEEKLY·NEWSPAPER

No. 710.—VOL. XXVIII.
 General Post Office as a Newspaper | SATURDAY, JULY 7, 1883 | WITH EXTRA SUPPLEMENT | PRICE SIXPENCE
 Or by Post Sixpence Half

THE KING'S VISIT TO EASTBOURNE, JULY 11ᵀᴴ 1903.

King Edward VII and Queen Alexandra came to Eastbourne for a few days in July 1903, staying at Compton Place.

Right: During his stay, the King visited the Princess Alice Memorial Hospital. He had been close to his sister Alice, who had nursed him when he had typhoid in 1871, and in 1899 he had donated an operating table to the hospital. 'I paid a "surprise" visit to the hospital at 9.30 this morning and found everything in admirable order, the wards being specially well ventilated.'

Opposite below: The Princess Alice Memorial Hospital was opened on 30 June 1883 by the Prince and Princess of Wales (later King Edward VII and Queen Alexandra). The opening was featured in *The Graphic*. Clockwise from top left: the procession from the station, a view of the hospital, the presentation of purses (because not quite enough money had been raised), and a welcoming arch made by the fishermen.

All Saints Convalescent Hospital in Meads, built in Gothic Revival style by Henry Woodyer, opened in 1869. The Bishop of Chichester, who didn't agree with women in the Church, declined to attend, so the Bishop of Winchester blessed it. (The chapel was consecrated in 1874 by a new Bishop of Chichester). The Sisters moved out in 1959. Used by the NHS mainly as a day hospital and stroke unit, it closed in 2004 and is now on the market.

The infirmary block of Eastbourne Workhouse, later St Mary's Hospital, was built in 1889; it was the first formal attempt to separate the fit and ill inmates. In 1989 the nearest part of the building housed Berwick and Dicker wards, with Cuckmere ward and the physiotherapy department in the far section. The Second World War ARP surface shelter, right, was used as a Red Cross Library store after the war. All the buildings were demolished in 1990.

Gildredge Hospital opened on 27 July 1914 as the town's TB hospital. It cost £2,143 to build plus £1,250 to purchase the site from the Davies-Gilberts. It was built at a remote edge of the town because TB was the plague of the age: deaths from it far exceeded those from cancer and of the first 1,000 patients in the hospital, 530 died. With antibiotics and other therapy, cases and deaths plummeted; 1968 was the first year with no TB deaths in Eastbourne. The hospital was razed to the ground in 1979 and Bodmin Close has now been built on the site.

Eastbourne workhouse staff, 1915. Porters and clerks stand at the back, ward maids and cooks in the third row. Sister Appleyard and Dr James Adams are seated in the second row. After 1919 workhouses were called 'institutions'. Eastbourne's institution became St Mary's Hospital in 1930 and went on become a well-respected hospital. The stigma, however, persisted into the middle of the twentieth century, when old folk would plead not to be sent into the 'pauper hospital'.

The staff of the Eastbourne Central Military Hospital, 1917. Between 1915 and 1920 the old workhouse (behind) was used to treat the war-wounded, particularly those with severe injuries. Mrs Ellen Bumstead, who nursed there, said, 'On 3 May 1916 the hospital was honoured with a visit by King George V and Queen Mary, accompanied by the Prince of Wales and Princess Mary, both in uniform. She looked so much the "English Rose" with her lovely complexion.'

All Saints Convalescent Hospital was taken over in January 1917 for the 16th Canadian Base Hospital. It was converted into a fully equipped hospital with its own operating theatre and X-ray, laboratory and pharmacy departments. Sadly, the hospital staff were helpless when faced with the influenza epidemic of 1918, when hundreds of Canadians died, including seventy at All Saints.

The laundry staff of the Poor Law Institution (later St Mary's Hospital), 1922. They worked long hours, were paid around £1 a week and they had to clear up their work area before they were allowed home.

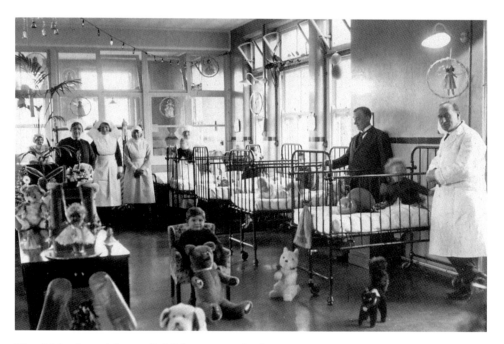

The children's ward (later called Selmeston ward) of St Mary's Hospital, 1930. Matron Mary Letheren is on the extreme left; on the right are the Medical Officer of Health, Dr William Willoughby, and (in the white coat) Dr Herbert McAleenan, a GP, Medical Superintendent and keen golfer at the Willingdon Club. When asked by a patient who had recently been treated for a heart attack whether it would be all right to play golf, he replied, 'Certainly. What better place to die than on a golf course?'

The doctor, matron and staff of the Isolation (later Downside) Hospital in 1904. The hospital dated from 1885 and was extended in 1905. 'My brothers were taken away to the fever hospital with diphtheria, and men lit a sulphur candle to fumigate the attic bedroom where we all slept and no-one could enter for three days. I thought it was fun until I went down with it myself and had all my toys burnt'. Matron Bailey hardly ever left the hospital and died in 1933 after over forty years in the post.

The Princess Alice Memorial Hospital X-ray department in 1925.

E ward (renamed East Dean ward after 1948) at St Mary's Hospital, Christmas 1935. In the centre are Staff Nurse D.M. Clarke and Sister Olerenshaw. The floors are shining and even in winter every fanlight window is open.

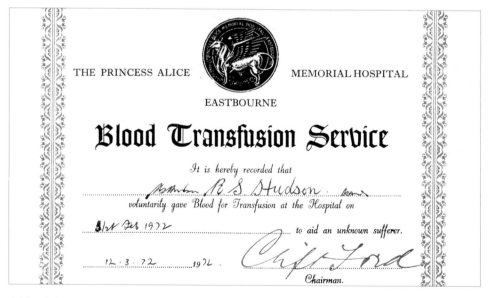

THE PRINCESS ALICE MEMORIAL HOSPITAL

EASTBOURNE

Blood Transfusion Service

It is hereby recorded that

R S Hudson

voluntarily gave Blood for Transfusion at the Hospital on

1st Feb 1972 to aid an unknown sufferer.

12 . 3 . 72 19*72* .

Chairman.

A blood donation certificate from the Princess Alice Memorial Hospital. In the 1920s and '30s, each hospital kept a list of donors to be called upon if needed, although the first call was often on the patient's relatives, who were more easily available. It was a cumbersome, inefficient and dangerous approach and was replaced by the National Blood Transfusion Service. When this was formed during the Second World War, it was soon recognised to be a much superior system.

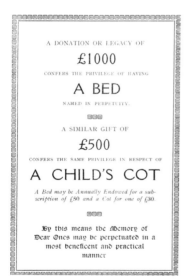

BATH REGULATIONS

All inmates are to be bathed at least once a YEAR (unless exempted by Medical Certificate), and oftener IF NECESSARY.

The Bath attendant ONLY is to prepare the Bath.

The COLD Water is to be turned on first

There must be 10 inches of water in the Bath.

The Water is never to be LESS than 80, or MORE than 98, degrees of heat. This is to be tested by the Thermometer (not by the HAND) before an Inmate be allowed to enter the Bath.

Inmates are not to be kept in the Bath more than TEN minutes unless absolutely necessary, and on no pretence whatever are their Heads to be put under Water.

After bathing, each inmate is to be dried and dressed as quickly as possible.

The Baths, Floor, Brushes, Combs, &c., are always to be left in proper condition for next day's use.

All wet Towels to be removed.

Above left: A flight of angels: nurses posing on the staircase of the new art deco nurses' home in 1941. The home was one of the few constructions allowed during the Second World War; permission was probably only granted because the nurses were looking after servicemen.

Above right: Instructions for bathing 'inmates' at an Eastbourne institution.

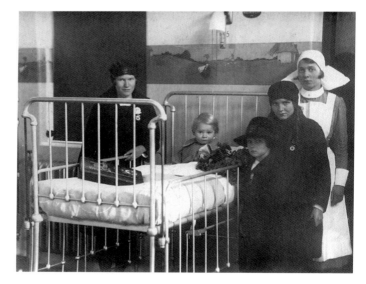

Before the creation of the NHS, at many hospitals it was possible to have a bed named after you if you gave a donation of, say, £1,000. In Eastbourne there was graduated scale of donations. The Girls' High School raised £50 in 1922 to provide a cot in the children's ward, and it was renewed annually until the Second World War. Pupils would visit and take presents for the patient occupying the cot at the time. Miriam Ash is on the left and the other two pupils are Evelyn Millward and, in front, Margaret Riddle.

St Mary's Hospital night staff on the flat roof of the nurses' home in 1943. From left to right, back row: Nurses Brazier, Postle, –?–, Glynne and Hemsley. Front row: Nurse O'Shea, Staff Nurse Wilkins and Nurse McKay. Some are wearing their tin hats, probably for fun, but workmen were machine-gunned by a German plane while the home was being built. The nurses with badges on their coats were from the Civil Nursing Reserve, who helped out during the war.

Ann Wood, aged 10, seen here with Sister Olive Hewitt (left) and Staff Nurse Mavis Constable on her birthday, 10 October 1952. She was the first patient at St Mary's Hospital to be cured of tuberculous meningitis after treatment with the antibiotic streptomycin. Previous cases had proved to be uniformly fatal; now, if treated in time, patients usually recover fully. Ann went on to live a normal life, to marry, run a shop and have children of her own.

'Upperton', at No. 9 Upperton Road, was taken over as a seventy-bed Red Cross Hospital in the First World War. The wards were named after war heroes and heroines such as Cavell, Beatty and Jellicoe. The Medical Officers gave their services free, there were two paid nurses and the rest were volunteers. These patients weren't the most seriously wounded and only one died out of 1,400. It became the Maternity Home in 1920, for 'married mothers only'. It was a step towards improving maternal mortality which at the time was about 1 in 250; another change from nowadays was that the mothers stayed in for an average of seventeen days – enjoying the rest. This picture was taken just before it was demolished to make way for Marlborough Court.

The Christmas babies in the St Mary's Hospital maternity ward, 1967. The staff wearing dark uniforms are, from left to right: Sister Elizabeth Hood, Sister Brenda Dant, Midwifery Superintendent Sheila Chad, Sister Florence Bedwell, Porter Harry Warriner and Sister Janet Williams. In 1976 the obstetric units moved to the new hospital in Kings Drive.

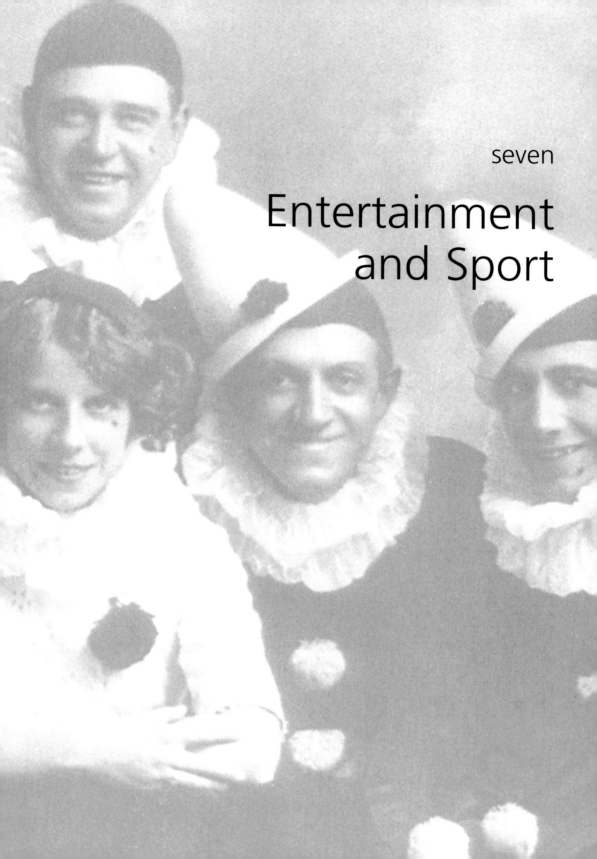

seven

Entertainment and Sport

After bathing, visitors to Eastbourne wanted to be entertained, so George Fisher's Library and Lounge at Nos 16-17 Marine Parade opened in 1784. John Heatherly was running it by 1817 and in his *A Description of Eastbourne and its Environs* he describes 'a goodly library, delightfully situated by the sea, with one of the best lodging houses, daily papers and periodicals. The Library is spacious and an excellent Billiard Table is for the use of gentlemen only'. It lasted with its two Georgian bay windows until 1948, having been damaged in the Second World War.

Above: South Street Theatre was Eastbourne's first, built for the Fisher family in 1798. It was situated opposite where the Dewdrop Inn stands today. The building was taken over as a carpenter's shop by the Haine family in 1838. It was demolished in the 1880s, by which time Haine's business had moved over the road.

Right: This playbill is for a performance of Sheridan's *The School for Scandal* on 19 October 1809.

FOR THE BENEFIT OF

Mr. & Mrs. Dormer.

THEATRE, EAST-BOURNE.

On THURSDAY Evening, OCT. 19, 1809, will be presented, a celebrated COMEDY, (written by R. B. Sheridan, Esq.) call'd,

THE

School for Scandal.

Sir Peter Teazle,   Mr. DORMER.
Sir Oliver Surface,   Mr. MORETON.
Joseph Surface,   Mr. RACKHAM.
Charles Surface,   Mr. AMTHOS.
Crabtree,   Mr. JONAS.
Sir Benjamin Backbite,   Mr. GEORGE.
Rowley,   Mr. GRIFFITH.
Careless, (with a Song)   Mr. BRANTON.
William,   Master RACKHAM.
Snake,   Mr. TAYLOR.
Mrs. Candour,   Mrs. NAYLOR.
Maria,   Mrs. BRANTON.
Lady Sneerwell,   Miss HOOPER.
And, Lady Teazle,   Mrs. DORMER.

END OF THE PLAY,
A favourite DANCE, by Miss HOOPER.
And, an IRISH SONG, by Mr. GRIFFITH.

To which will be added, the favourite musical Farce, (not acted here these 3 years) of

My Grandmother.

Sir Matthew Medley,   Mr. STACKWOOD.
Vapour,   Mr. AMTHOS.
Souffrance,   Mr. TAYLOR
James,   Master RACKHAM.
Dicky Gossip,   Mr. JONAS.
Charlotte,   Miss HOOPER.
And, Florella, (My Grandmother)   Mrs. DORMER.

BOXES, 3s.——PIT and SLIPS, 2s.——GALLERY, 1s.
Tickets to be had at the Library; New Inn; Lamb Inn; and of Mr. and Mrs. Dormer, at Mr. Adam's, carpenter, Bedger Square; and at the Theatre, where Places for the Boxes may be taken.
Doors to be opened at SIX, and to begin at SEVEN o'clock.
No Person can be admitted behind the Scenes.

Nights of performing, will be Tuesdays, Thursdays, and Saturdays.

Lewes: Printed by W. and A. Lee.

Devonshire Park Theatre, designed by Henry Currey, opened in 1884 with a performance of T.T.W. Robertson's *David Garrick*. After a makeover by Frank Matcham in 1903, H. Clunn described it as 'one of the finest on the South Coast'. Having leased it for five years, the council bought it in February 1957 for £33,750. The Italianate towers contained water tanks.

The Devonshire Park complex was designed for 'high-class recreation' to extend the holiday season. The Devonshire Swimming Baths opened in 1874. Built by G.A. Wallis, they were the largest heated salt-water baths in the country. The Floral Hall opened in 1875 and the Pavilion the next year. Devonshire Park soon had a music garden and facilities for cricket, tennis, racquets, roller skating and cycling – including a Ladies' Cycling Academy. The Winter Garden, which holds 1,600 people, is used for exhibitions and balls.

The Duke of Devonshire's Orchestra gave its first concert at the Winter Garden in 1876, under conductor Julian Adams. After he died in 1887, Norfolk Megone conducted during the summer and Pierre Tas during the winter. In 1900 the orchestra had over fifty players and set the tone in musical entertainment, appearing with many instrumentalists and vocalists, from Fritz Kreisler to Clara Butt. It was taken over by the council after the First World War. Captain Henry Amers, the Director of Music 1920-36, cut a fine figure and established a first-rate tradition of classical and military music.

Around 1900, 'The Minstrels gave two performances a day and there was a Punch and Judy show on the pier'. By 1910 the Minstrels were being gradually replaced by Pierrot concert troops.

The Olympian Concert Party, who performed on Eastbourne Pier during the summer of 1913.

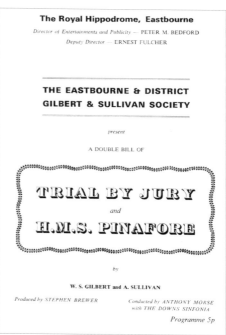

The Royal Hippodrome, Eastbourne

Director of Entertainments and Publicity — PETER M. BEDFORD
Deputy Director — ERNEST FULCHER

**THE EASTBOURNE & DISTRICT
GILBERT & SULLIVAN SOCIETY**

present

A DOUBLE BILL OF

TRIAL BY JURY

and

H.M.S. PINAFORE

by

W. S. GILBERT and A. SULLIVAN

Produced by STEPHEN BREWER   *Conducted by* ANTHONY MORSE
with THE DOWNS SINFONIA

Programme 5p

Above left: The Manhattan cinema (previously Mansells New Central) after its closure in 1966. Between the wars, Eastbourne, like every other town, had a love affair with 'the pictures'. Astaire Avenue was even named after film star Fred Astaire's sister, who married a member of the local Cavendish family.

Above right: The Royal Hippodrome Theatre, built in 1883 and now owned by the council, continues to put on popular shows.

Between 1954 and 1969 Eastbourne had a miniature tramway. The Crumbles Tramway ran from Royal Parade, past Princes Park to the Crumbles. It was extended in 1959, but moved to Seaton in Devon ten years later. The Dotto train started here in 1988. Three trains – *Romeo, Juliet* and *Cupid* – operate in season along the front from the Sovereign Centre to Holywell.

The 1,600-seat Congress Theatre was opened by Princess Margaret in 1963. This typical 1960s building has been listed. In 1955 the council contemplated building a new conference and concert hall in place of the Wish Tower, but finally put it on the site of the Indian Pavilion at Devonshire Park.

Devonshire Park's first tennis tournament was held in 1881; now the Devonshire Park Women's Lawn Tennis Championship attracts top players from all over the world. Martina Navratilova won the title eleven times; Kim Clijsters was the winner in 2005. The arena has a seating capacity of 7,500.

eight

Education and Schools

Eastbourne College, showing the west front with Memorial Tower. The college opened in 1867 in Spencer Road and moved into Henry Currey's College House in Blackwater Road in 1871. The college chapel opened in June 1874. During the Second World War, the college was taken over by the armed forces and the pupils were evacuated to Radley. The college has been greatly extended since the war. Girls first entered in 1969 and the college took over the Beresford House School grounds in 1994. Famous alumni include Nobel Laureate Frederick Soddy, Sir Hugh Casson, Woodrow Wyatt, John Wells and Eddie Izzard.

Moira House Girls' School, Upper Carlisle Road was founded in Croydon by Charles Ingham in 1875 and came to Eastbourne in 1887. The school took over neighbouring Boston House School. Former pupils include Prunella Scales and Rumer Godden.

South Lynn was a boys' school from 1880-1914, was used an RNAS Mess during the First World War and later became a girls' school. It was demolished in 1930s and South Lynn Close was built on the site. Captain Lawrence Oates (1880-1912), of Antarctic fame, was a pupil at the boys' school. There was a plaque in his memory in St Anne's church until it was bombed in the Second World War.

St Cyprian's School, founded in 1900, had an outstanding record, thanks to Mrs Vaughan Wilkes, the headmaster's wife, who was known as 'Mum'. The boys endured a spartan regime, with a pre-breakfast plunge and run round the field whatever the weather. One old boy said, 'I spent four years in a German POW Camp, but my time at St Cyprian's had prepared me well'. In 1916 the school's Classics prize was won by Eric Blair (George Orwell), the English prize by Cyril Connolly, the Arithmetic prize by Henry Longhurst and the Drawing prize by Cecil Beaton.

The Technical Institute, on the site of today's Central Library. It held a library, a museum, a continuation school and art school. It was bombed on 4 June 1943 and moved to St Anne's Road, reopening in the same year. It moved to Cross Levels Way in 1997 and is now Sussex Downs College.

Above left: Author and journalist Cyril Connolly (1903-74), attended St Cyprian's School and retired to St John's Road, where there is a plaque. His writings include *The Rock Pool* (1935), *Enemies of Promise* (1938), which contains material about his prep school, and *The Missing Diplomats* (1953).

Above right: A 1924 school report from St Mary's Church Girls' School.

The Links, Meads. It was built by G.A. Wallis in 1869 and Miss Potts, a former royal governess, ran a school here between 1908 and 1925. Miss Potts' hair was drawn into a bun, prompting the royal children to call her Cowpat. When the Countess of Athlone (a granddaughter of Queen Victoria) sent her daughter to the school, the royal patronage attracted pupils such as (Lady) Edwina Mountbatten, (Dame) Felicity Hyde and Rachel Wrey (Lady Willoughby de Brooke). In the 1930s The Links became a holiday centre for the Methodist Guild and was used as an Emergency Rest and Feeding Centre for bombed-out families during the Second World War. It was sold for development in 1998.

Four wealthy Victorian ladies ran infants' elementary schools to keep the cost off the ratepayers. Blanche, Countess of Burlington (1812-40), who was the wife of the seventh Duke of Devonshire, opened the first school, in Meads Road in 1836. Lydia Brodie (1815-91) provided the second in 1853; it is now Flint Halls in Old Town. The third, opened by Julia Brodie (1814-72), was the infants' school next to Christ Church in Seaside. The fourth school was opened by Maria Brodie (1807-92) in 1890; it is the only one of the four that continues as a school and is now Meads County Primary School in Rownsley Road.

The
Eastbourne School of
Domestic Economy

☯

November 22nd, 1935

Left: An invitation card for the 1935 Christmas Dinner at the prestigious Eastbourne School of Domestic Economy. Elise Orange Randall (1885–1959), known as Ranny, started the school with £5 in the bank in 1907. The fees in 1912 were 24 guineas (£25.20) per term. The girls came for a year at the age of 18 and boarded at the school; in the early days, some brought their personal maids. The Royal Navy commandeered the school in 1940; Randall stayed and cooked for the sailors of 'HMS *Ranny*' throughout the war. The school reopened after the war, with the students now wanting a career in catering. It closed in 1996.

Below: The first fifteen girls at the Municipal Girls' School (later the High School) in 1903, with Miss Ekman, the French mistress. To keep the rates down, Eastbourne was one of only two authorities that did not have a School Board. Children who didn't go to a private school went to church schools, which were good but had insufficient places. With the Education Act of 1902, the council had to provide schooling; Willowfield School was the first to open and this school followed.

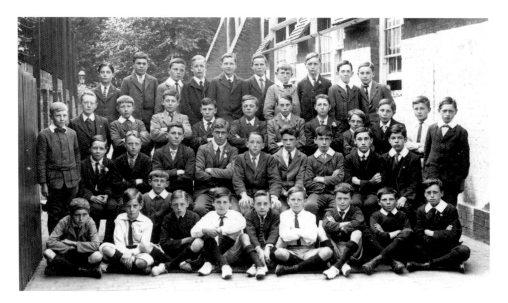

The upper school of St Saviour's Choir School in Furness Road, 1914. St Mary's Church School had functioned near the church tower from around 1750. The Revd Alexander Brodie founded the new St Mary's School in Church Street in 1814, which admitted girls from 1816 (eventually becoming a Girls' County School in 1952). Holy Trinity Church School, and later a Methodist and a Roman Catholic school followed.

The 1944 Form V at the High School. The school moved from Upperton Road to the new building in Eldon Road in 1939. It wasn't long before the pupils were evacuated to Hitchin; they dribbled back to Eastbourne from 1942. The school is now Cavendish School.

The staffroom at the Girls' High School, 1950. Miss Lois Gunnery was the headmistress from 1933-69. At that time, most of the teachers were unmarried and devoted their lives to their 'gals'.

The Guides of the Girls' High School celebrate Empire Day (24 May, Queen Victoria's birthday) in 1946 by singing a Maori song at Compton Place. Empire Day was celebrated at every school from around 1903 until the 1940s, with dressing-up, parades and sports. In 1937 over 4,000 schoolchildren marched past the mayor at Gildredge Park. 'At school we paraded waving our Union flags and singing patriotic songs – and we had a half-day holiday so it was grand.'

nine

Wartime

Part of the line of Martello towers built between 1804 and 1812 to defend against invasion by Napoleon. The towers were positioned to provide covering fire over the flat coastline between Eastbourne and Pevensey. They were later used by the coastguard, as residences and for target practice, and some have been lost to the sea. The Redoubt Fortress in Royal Parade was built to act as a fort and depot for the towers. The fort and some of the towers were brought back into active service during the Second World War.

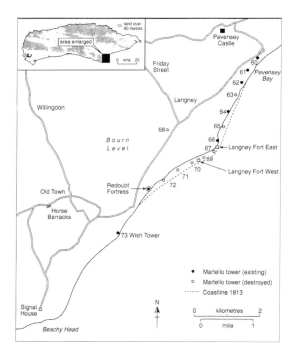

Above left: A map showing the sites of the Martello towers between Eastbourne and Pevensey.

Above right: Officers of the Cinque Ports Volunteers in a painting by R.J. Marrion. Most of the small British regular army was overseas during the Napoleonic Wars, so the majority of the troops defending the coast were militia or volunteers.

During the First World War, 1,000 residents died in the forces and 50 ships were sunk by U-boats off Beachy Head. There were still plenty of visitors to the town and it hosted Summerdown Camp, a military convalescent hospital, the largest of its kind in Europe. The first convalescent troops, the 'Blue Boys', arrived in April 1915 and by the time the camp closed in February 1920, almost 150,000 had passed through, with 90 per cent returned to active duties. The troops had film shows on Sundays, which were strictly not allowed elsewhere in the town. The main pathway through the camp became Old Camp Road.

In 1939 Eastbourne was declared a Safe Zone and received evacuees. However, in 1940 Eastbourne found itself right in the front line and many people left. The town's first taste of conflict was in March 1940, when the 5,000-ton *Barnhill* was bombed off Beachy Head and drifted ashore near Langney Point. The lifeboat rescued the survivors.

During the Second World War, Eastbourne once more succoured the wounded; these Dunkirk survivors are recovering at St Mary's Hospital. A nurse recounted how she was confronted with bloodstained helmets, packs and rifles: 'The sight of C ward packed tight with soldiers will remain with me forever. They were only boys of 18, 19 and 20, and I was only 20. One lad with a bullet in his brain thought I was an angel when I gave him a drink. He died the next day'.

Bomb damage in Arlington Road on 27 September 1940; there is a gush of water from the mains in the middle of the road. The first phase of serious action was from July 1940 to June 1941, with the Battle of Britain raging overhead and daytime raids by bombers. There was also sporadic night bombing, mainly from planes damaged on their way to London, who jettisoned their bombs to assist their return to France.

Above left: Many Eastbourne residents were ex-servicemen and they flocked to join the Local Defence Volunteers, later called the Home Guard.

Above right: The corner house in Latimer Road after 15 September 1940, Battle of Britain Day. As so often, the blast effects could be weird; most of the house has gone but a bed and a dressing table with ewer stay precariously balanced.

The tennis courts at Devonshire Park were bombed, perhaps by one of the returning planes emptying its bomb-bay. Notice how little damage is caused when bombs land in soft earth.

Cavendish Place, 28 September 1940, was the scene of extreme bravery. The bombing left eight people trapped in a basement and rescue squads strove to reach them, hampered by a burst water main and an unexploded bomb. They extracted five and another, a 17-year-old girl, was taken out after both her legs had been amputated; sadly, she died in hospital two days later.

Above left: On 31 August 1940, there was a loud bang at around 5.00 p.m in Wish Road, with no aircraft in sight. During the clearing-up operation, remnants of a 4in shell were found. German records found after the war confirmed that a U-boat had shelled the town.

Above right: This bus was raked by cannon and machine-gun fire from 'hit-and-run' fighter-bombers. Not surprisingly, the driver was killed.

Above and right: On 8 October 1940 a 250kg bomb fell on North Street, just behind Dale & Kerley's store (now T.J. Hughes'), but did not explode – a 'UXB' as they were termed. A few days later, a bomb disposal squad began digging for the bomb. The next morning, the bomb was fully exposed (above right). The detonator (the white spot) was found to be jammed and impossible to remove, so the UXB had to be dug out and transported away live. Intrepid press photographer Wilf Bignell photographed every phase of the highly dangerous procedure.

Right: Pulling out the live bomb.

Below: Another UXB having its detonator removed. Bombs failed to explode because the bomb aimer had failed to prime them, or they were delayed-action bombs timed to go off around three hours after the raid, to disrupt rescue work, or they were booby-trapped to blow up anyone brave enough to attempt to defuse them. Sergeant Hoare of this Royal Engineers squad and a policeman, Sergeant Owens, were killed by a UXB on 26 October 1940, near the present Ashford Road car park.

The next frightening phase of the air attacks were the hit-and-run raids in 1942-43. These were low-level attacks by fighter-bombers, who dropped bombs with great accuracy and sprayed the town with gunfire before zooming back across the Channel. This was Barclays Bank in Terminus Road before the Second World War; it had remained unchanged since it was Lewes Old Bank in 1896.

It was a very different scene after the bombing of 7 March 1943, when the building was effectively destroyed.

The replacement Barclays Bank nears completion in 1958; it looks much the same today from the outside. The inside has been completely altered, with open counters replaced by queuing lanes and security screens.

Eastbourne's worst single incident was when a surface shelter, designed to protect against bomb splinters and blast, took a direct hit from a 250kg bomb on 3 April 1943. This is the junction of Spencer Road and South Street and, apart from rubble, nothing is left of the shelter; all those sheltering inside died. Thirty-three were killed in the raid and ninety-nine injured.

The Ministry of Information did their best to keep up morale on the home front. This charming Newbould poster shows the Beachy Head Downs, with Belle Tout near the centre.

Charleston Road after a flying bomb (V1) on 18 June 1944. The last phase of the air attacks were the V1s or doodlebugs. The first was seen from Beachy Head, on the night of 12-13 June, heading for London. London was the target for most of these bombs; Eastbourne and the South Coast only received malfunctioning or misdirected ones. Only fifteen landed in the borough and although they caused a great deal of damage to property and many civilians were injured, none died. Only one V2 landed within the borough, thankfully on isolated farmland.

The end of the war in Europe was greeted with relief in May 1945. Street parties were the rule as people gathered together something out of the rations to give the children a day to remember. This is Kingston Road, Hampden Park but there were celebrations everywhere.

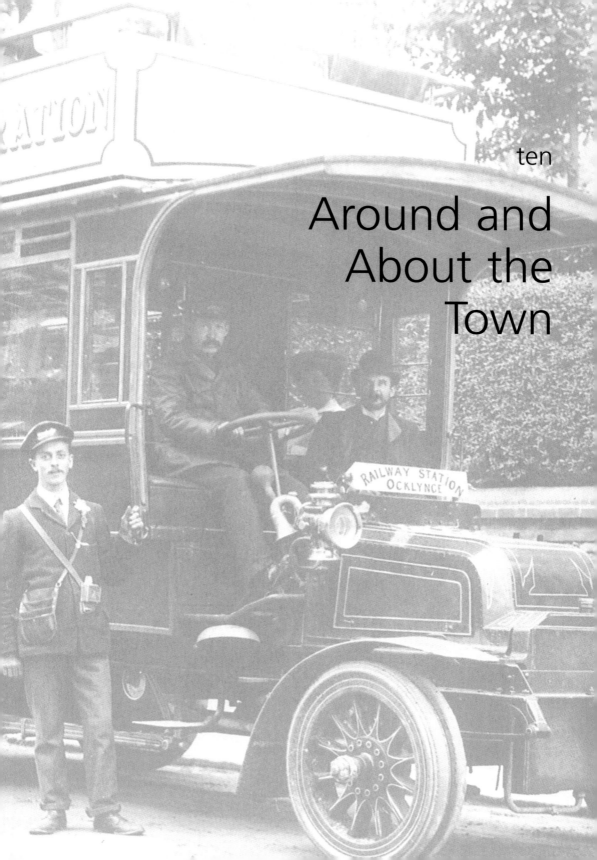

ten

Around and About the Town

Compton Place (above left) was bought by Spencer Compton MP (later Earl of Wilmington) in 1724. It was Bourne Place when built by farmer James Burton shortly after he acquired 280 acres in 1555. In 1780 the owner was Lady Elizabeth Compton (above right); she was an unmarried woman of 20, her parents having died of tuberculosis. When she married Lord George Cavendish in 1782, her lands went into the Cavendish (Dukes of Devonshire) family, and so the Cavendishes came to Eastbourne, and they eventually owned two-thirds of the town.

Pilgrims, in Borough Lane by the old Saxon crossroads, is the oldest house in the town. It is a Wealden house, to which is attached a one-up, one-down cottage. The features of the house, which has no foundations, include solars, fourteenth-century jettying and cellars in solid chalk dating from around 1130. A plaque on the wall commemorates the visits of Charles Dickens to the house.

Langney Priory, in a 1785 painting by Lambert. It was probably a farming grange belonging to the Cluniac Priory at Lewes and incorporates a small chapel and a refectory, with a dormitory above. Since the 1950s, it has been surrounded by new housing estates. It is now privately owned and is well worth a visit.

The Lamb inn near St Mary's church in Old Town is a medieval timbered building with a vaulted undercroft. In the 1780s the outside was given a fashionable Georgian rendering, which was removed following an accident with a runaway horse in 1912, revealing the original black and white timbering, which is what you see today. Its sixteenth-century timbers lie over an Early English cellar which has a central roof boss of a style common in the fourteenth century. The stories about underground passages appear to be just tales. The Lamb provided an assembly room and a ballroom for visitors of note, particularly during the Napoleonic Wars. It was here that Charles Dickens, in Eastbourne to visit Augustus Egg in 1831, acted in amateur dramatics.

Terminus Road, *c.* 1900. On the left is the station, Eastbourne's third, with its waiting carriages. When the railway came to Eastbourne in May 1849, the band played 'Behold the Conquering Hero Comes' and there were speeches, greasy poles and fireworks which went on all day. The day certainly changed the town forever. Terminus Road was laid out by John Davies-Gilbert in 1851.

The Town Hall, 2003. It was opened in 1886 after arguments about the site, the builder and the cost. The gold-tipped tower by Gillett & Johnson had space for a four-dial clock and bells, but it wasn't until noon on 11 July 1892 that the mayor started the £700 Westminster chiming clock. The chimes are Cambridge quarters.

The Gilbert Arms (known as the Squirrel) was Hartfield Farmhouse until the railway came. Pianist and composer Sir William Sterndale Bennett (1816-75), who often came to the town, wrote his cantata 'The May Queen' in 1858 in the bay-window room on the left.

The Princess Alice tree, c. 1900. This is where the war memorial stands today. In the centre is H.R. Browne's dispensing chemists, which occupied these premises from 1860 to 1976. On the extreme left is the shop of draper and silk merchant Henry Evenden, at the corner of South Street and Cornfield Terrace. The premises became Dickeson & French, and, from 1991, the furnisher David Salmon. The spire of St Saviour's can be seen on the left.

A 1904 Milnes–Daimler omnibus in Ocklynge. Eastbourne's municipal bus service was one of the earliest in the country, commencing in 1903.

A boat trip round the bay or to Beachy Head and back is a good way to see Eastbourne and learn more about the town.

The Arndale Centre officially opened on 7 October 1980, transforming shopping habits in Eastbourne. The name comes from the founders of a property trust, *Arn*old Hagenbach and Sam Chippen*dale*. There was a £4 million refurbishment in 1997, giving natural light on the walkways. Shops in Seaside Road and Grove Road are only just recovering now, and there is talk of extending the Arndale over the station.

To end this book, here are a few questions about the town. You can see this golden finial (above left) every day in Eastbourne, but where? This arch (above right) lies stranded in a Meads housing estate; what is it? While looking around the town, you can be seeking out a cabman's shelter in The Avenue, and the licence plates scattered all around the town but especially in King Edwards Parade.

Other local titles published by Tempus

Hastings Revisited

SUSAN E. KING

This pictorial history traces some of the developments that have taken place in the fishing community of Hastings from the late nineteenth century up to the Second World War. Illustrated with over 200 pictures, mostly drawn from the archives of Hastings Central Library, this volume highlights some of the important events that have occurred in the town, from the growth of tourism to the amalgamation of Hastings and St Leonards.

0 7524 3543 4

Brighton and Hove Cinemas

ALLEN EYLES

This fascinating collection of over 150 photographs provides a unique view of the cinemas of Brighton and Hove. In 1896 Brighton became the first town outside London to show films and it has had a remarkable range of picture houses over the years. These include the Regent, the most spectacular cinema in the country when it opened in 1921, and the Astoria, with its French Art Deco interior.

0 7524 3069 6

Bexhill-on-Sea The Second Selection

JULIAN PORTER

This fascinating second selection of old photographs from the collection of Bexhill Museum provides a glimpse of life in Bexhill during the late nineteenth and twentieth centuries. This collection of over 230 archive images includes Bexhill street scenes and seafront, the Old Town, Sidley and Little Common. Key events are recalled, including the opening of the Town Hall in 1895 and Britain's first motor car races on the seafront.

0 7524 2627 3

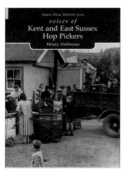

Voices of Kent and East Sussex Hop Pickers

HILARY HEFFERNAN

Right up to the late 1950s, the annual hop-picking season provided a welcome escape for thousands of families who lived and worked in the poorer parts of London, who would migrate every year to the hop gardens of Kent and Sussex to pick the harvest. The photographs and reminiscences in this book tell a fascinating story; of hardship, adventures, mishaps, misfortune and laughter experienced during hardworking holidays among the bines.

0 7524 3240 0

If you are interested in purchasing other books published by Tempus, or in case you have difficulty finding any Tempus books in your local bookshop, you can also place orders directly through our website
www.tempus-publishing.com